S0-BRB-272

ALIA'S MISSION

SAVING THE BOOKS OF IRAQ
Inspired by a True Story

MARK ALAN STAMATY

HAMPTON-BROWN

THE EXCHANGE

What is worth saving?

For Janet Schulman

Alia's Mission by Mark Alan Stamaty. Copyright © 2004 by Mark Alan Stamaty. Cover illustration copyright © 2004 by Mark Alan Stamaty. Published by arrangement with Random House Children's Books, a division of Random House, Inc. New York, New York, U.S.A. All rights reserved.

On-Page Coach ™ (introductions, questions, on-page glossaries), The Exchange, back cover summary © Hampton-Brown.

All rights reserved. No part of this book may be reproduced or transmitted in any form or by any means, electronic or mechanical, including photocopying, recording, or by any information storage and retrieval system, without permission in writing from the publisher.

Hampton-Brown
P.O. Box 223220
Carmel, California 93922
800-333-3510
www.hampton-brown.com

Printed in the United States of America

ISBN-13: 978-0-7362-2802-2
ISBN-10: 0-7362-2802-0

06 07 08 09 10 11 12 13 14 10 9 8 7 6 5 4 3

PERFORMING HUMANLY IMPOSSIBLE FEATS
doing things that real people cannot do

TROUBLED NATION country with many problems

DICTATOR person who leads the country alone

AMID GROWING FEARS OF WAR People are afraid
of war, but

Alia loves her job as a librarian in Basra, Iraq. When she hears that there will be a war, she worries about the books.

EVERY MORNING, ALIA DRIVES TO WORK. OFTEN, SHE WORRIES ABOUT THE PROBLEMS OF THE WORLD, BUT DEEP IN HER HEART IS A FEELING OF JOY.

ALIA LOVES HER JOB...

...AS CHIEF LIBRARIAN OF BASRA CENTRAL LIBRARY...

...SURROUNDED BY HER FAVORITE THINGS OF ALL: BOOKS!

DEEP IN HER HEART IS Alia's job gives her
SURROUNDED BY working with

EVER SINCE ALIA WAS A LITTLE GIRL, BOOKS HAVE BEEN A SOURCE OF HAPPINESS AND ADVENTURE FOR HER.

BOOKS HAVE TAUGHT HER ABOUT MANY THINGS, LIKE THE LONG AND FASCINATING HISTORY OF THE VERY LAND SHE LIVES ON...

...OF MANY TRIBES AND CIVILIZATIONS, OF KINGS AND CONQUERORS SINCE ANCIENT TIMES.

BEEN A SOURCE OF HAPPINESS AND ADVENTURE FOR HER made her happy and helped her to imagine things

VERY same

TRIBES AND CIVILIZATIONS different groups of people and ways of living

ANCIENT TIMES a long time ago

FROM BOOKS, ALIA HAS LEARNED ABOUT THE RISE OF THE GREAT MUSLIM CIVILIZATION 1,300 YEARS AGO, WHICH BUILT ASTONISHING CITIES AND LED THE WHOLE WORLD IN TRADE, SCIENCE, AND CULTURE.

AND BOOKS HAVE TAUGHT HER, TOO, OF THE FRIGHTFUL MONGOL INVASION 500 YEARS LATER, WHICH ENDED THAT CELEBRATED ERA AND BROUGHT THE DESTRUCTION BY FIRE OF THE GREAT BAGHDAD LIBRARY AND THE LOSS OF ITS IRREPLACEABLE TREASURES.

RISE growth

ASTONISHING amazing

LED THE WHOLE WORLD IN TRADE made amazing discoveries in business

CELEBRATED ERA incredible time period

IRREPLACEABLE TREASURES books that could not be replaced

BEFORE YOU MOVE ON...

1. **Fact and Opinion** Reread page 3. Which statements are facts and which are opinions?

2. **Summarize** Why are books so important to Alia?

LOOK AHEAD Read pages 8–10 to find out why Alia is worried.

MADE A PAINFUL IMPRESSION ON ALIA made
Alia feel very sad

VOLUMES books

FEEL FREE TO Please

STILL, WITH EACH NEW REPORT OF THE COMING INVASION, ALIA'S WORRIES INCREASE.

OFTEN, SHE DISCUSSES HER FEARS WITH HER HUSBAND.

I'M SO AFRAID OF SOMETHING BAD HAPPENING TO THE LIBRARY ...WAR CAN SO EASILY GET OUT OF CONTROL....

WITH ONE BOMB OR ONE FIRE, ALL THOSE BOOKS COULD BE DESTROYED... JUST LIKE THE GREAT LIBRARY OF BAGHDAD!

WE CAN'T LET THAT HAPPEN!

I KNOW! I'LL GO TO THE GOVERNMENT!

WITH EACH NEW REPORT OF THE COMING INVASION every time she sees on the news that a war will start soon

GET OUT OF CONTROL destroy cities and damage treasures

GO TO THE GOVERNMENT ask if the government will help me

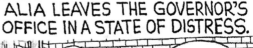

APPEARS UNIMPRESSED looks like he is not interested

YOUR REQUEST IS DECLINED. You cannot move the books.

RECORDS OF information about

COLLECTIVE MEMORY memories

IN A STATE OF DISTRESS worried and sad

BEFORE YOU MOVE ON...

1. **Conclusions** Alia is worried that the library in Basra will be destroyed. Why?

2. **Main Idea and Details** Reread page 10. Alia believes books are worth saving. What details support this main idea?

LOOK AHEAD What happens to the library when the war begins? Read pages 11–15 to find out.

SWARMS WITH GOVERNMENT OFFICIALS
WHO'VE SET UP OPERATIONS TO HELP
COORDINATE THE WAR is full of people from the
government who are planning attacks
IN THE EYES OF THE WORLD to other countries

ALL DAY LONG, ALIA THINKS ABOUT WHAT TO DO. BY LATE AFTERNOON, SHE HAS AN IDEA.

AT QUITTING TIME, ALIA GOES TO A SHELF IN A BACK CORNER AND FILLS HER HANDBAG WITH BOOKS. THEN SHE HIDES TWO MORE ARMFULS UNDER HER SHAWL.

BEARING THE BULKY LOAD, SHE WALKS AS NORMALLY AS POSSIBLE PAST THE GOVERNMENT WORKERS, DOWN THE HALLWAY, THROUGH THE LOBBY, AND OUT OF THE LIBRARY.

BY THE TIME SHE REACHES HER CAR, HER ARMS AND SHOULDERS ARE ACHING KNOTS, HER HANDS NUMB AND TINGLY.

AT QUITTING TIME When she finishes working

BEARING THE BULKY LOAD Carrying the heavy books

HER ARMS AND SHOULDERS ARE ACHING KNOTS, HER HANDS NUMB AND TINGLY
she feels tired and sore

SHE LOOKS ALL AROUND HER TO MAKE SURE NO ONE IS WATCHING, THEN LOADS THE BOOKS INTO THE TRUNK AND GOES BACK FOR MORE.

THE GOVERNMENT WORKERS— PREOCCUPIED WITH THE WAR—TAKE LITTLE NOTICE OF THE COMINGS AND GOINGS OF A FEMALE LIBRARIAN.

IN SEVERAL TRIPS, ALIA MANAGES TO FILL THE TRUNK AND BACKSEAT, COVERING THE BOOKS CAREFULLY WITH A RUG AND A SHAWL. THEN SHE DRIVES HOME.

HER HUSBAND HELPS HER CARRY THE BOOKS INTO THEIR HOUSE. THEY STACK THEM NEATLY IN THE CLOSET.

TO MAKE SURE to see that

PREOCCUPIED WITH only thinking about

TAKE LITTLE NOTICE OF THE COMINGS AND GOINGS OF A FEMALE LIBRARIAN do not watch Alia going in and out

MANAGES is able to

ANOTHER CARFUL OF BOOKS enough books to fill
her car

OVERFLOWING very full

LINE fill

WHO AM I KIDDING?! I will not be able to do it!

BEFORE YOU MOVE ON...

1. **Conclusions** Reread page 11. Why does Saddam put an anti-aircraft gun on the library?

2. **Problem and Solution** The library is in danger. What is Alia's solution?

LOOK AHEAD Read pages 16–21 to find out why people are running around and stealing.

A FEW DAYS LATER, HER FEAR IS CONFIRMED AS BRITISH TROOPS ROAR INTO BASRA.

SHE LOOKS OUT HER WINDOW. PEOPLE ARE RUNNING ABOUT WILDLY IN THE STREETS.

ALIA CALLS THE LIBRARY. THE PHONE RINGS AND RINGS. WITH EVERY RING, HER HEART BEATS FASTER.

FINALLY, THE PHONE IS ANSWERED BY THE LIBRARY CUSTODIAN.

ALL THE SOLDIERS AND GOVERNMENT WORKERS LEFT THIS MORNING. THERE'S NO ONE HERE BUT ME...

...AND THE LOOTERS OUTSIDE.

NO ONE'S GUARDING THE LIBRARY!

HER FEAR IS CONFIRMED AS BRITISH TROOPS ROAR INTO BASRA British soldiers come to Basra, as Alia had feared

ABOUT around

LIBRARY CUSTODIAN man who cleans and watches the library

LOOTERS thieves

NEXT MORNING AT FIRST LIGHT **Early in the
morning**

THE STREETS ARE IN CHAOS **There is confusion**

LOADED DOWN WITH STOLEN GOODS **carrying
things they have stolen**

AT LAST   finally

GONE ARE   They stole

FIXTURES   furniture

WHO KNOWS WHAT ELSE   many other things

THERE'S NO TIME TO WASTE. Alia starts working immediately.

CONTACT call

SAYS A FEW WORDS tells the people why they need to save the books

HAVE A CHANCE might be able

A SHORT WHILE LATER, THEY SWING INTO ACTION.

ONE GROUP REMOVES BOOKS FROM THE SHELVES AND STACKS THEM CAREFULLY BY THE BACK DOOR OF THE LIBRARY.

A SECOND GROUP CARRIES THEM OUTSIDE TO A HIGH WALL THAT SEPARATES THE LIBRARY PROPERTY FROM ANIS'S RESTAURANT.

THE BOOKS ARE HANDED OVER THE WALL TO A THIRD GROUP, WHICH CARRIES THEM INTO THE RESTAURANT, PLACING THEM IN TALL STACKS.

IT IS A VERY BIG JOB. THEY WORK ALL DAY AND ALL NIGHT. IN THE LIGHT OF DAWN, THEY ARE STILL WORKING. EVERYONE IS TIRED, BUT THEY STAY AT IT, SPURRED ON BY DISTANT SOUNDS OF WAR.

SWING INTO ACTION start to work

LIGHT OF DAWN morning

**STAY AT IT, SPURRED ON BY DISTANT
SOUNDS OF WAR** keep working, because they
are worried about the war

PROGRESSES continues

PASSERSBY people walking by the library

I'M HEADED FOR THE LIBRARY TO LEND A HAND. I am going to the library to help.

BEFORE YOU MOVE ON...

1. **Cause and Effect** British tanks enter Basra. What happens to the city and the library next?

2. **Conclusions** Reread pages 20–21. Why do so many people join Alia to save the books?

LOOK AHEAD Read pages 22–27 to find out what makes Alia scream "No!" in the middle of the night.

EXACTLY! I'm not surprised!

THE STRAIN IN ALIA that Alia is very tired

OUGHT TO TAKE A BREAK should rest for a while

CLOUDS OF SMOKE FROM THE EXPLOSION FILL THE AIR.

I'LL SLEEP TONIGHT. RIGHT NOW, EVERY MINUTE COUNTS.

THEY WORK TILL CLOSE TO MIDNIGHT, THEN CALL IT A DAY.

GOOD NIGHT, ALIA. SEE YOU IN THE MORNING.

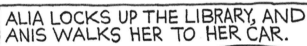

ALIA LOCKS UP THE LIBRARY, AND ANIS WALKS HER TO HER CAR.

I WISH I HAD THE STRENGTH TO WORK ALL NIGHT AGAIN TONIGHT AND EVERY NIGHT TILL ALL THE BOOKS ARE SAFE!

YOU'RE ONLY HUMAN, ALIA. YOU'RE DOING THE BEST YOU CAN.

THREE HOURS LATER, SHE IS SOUND ASLEEP, DREAMING OF BOOKS, WHEN THE PHONE RINGS....

...hello...

NO!!

THE LIBRARY'S ON FIRE! I'VE GOT TO GET THERE RIGHT AWAY!

I'LL DRIVE YOU.

EVERY MINUTE COUNTS we must do everything we can

CALL IT A DAY go home

YOU'RE ONLY HUMAN You need to rest sometimes

SOUND ASLEEP sleeping

WHO'S IN CHARGE?! Who is trying to stop the fire?!
BEINGS creatures

THE FLAMES RAGE ON, DEVOURING THE REST OF THE LIBRARY UNTIL ALL THAT'S LEFT IS A HEAP OF CASCADING ASH SURROUNDED BY A HOLLOW FRAME.

IT'S OVER, ALIA. YOU'RE EXHAUSTED. COME TO THE RESTAURANT. I'LL MAKE YOU SOME TEA.

LATER:

IF ONLY WE HAD MORE TIME... IF ONLY...

ARE YOU ALL RIGHT, DEAR? WHAT IS IT?!...

I FEEL...SO... DIZZY....

YOU'D BETTER LIE DOWN. THERE'S A COT IN THE BACK....

THE MEN TAKE ALIA TO THE HOSPITAL. A DOCTOR EXAMINES HER AND COMES OUT TO SPEAK WITH THEM.

SHE'S HAD A STROKE. SHE'LL NEED A LOT OF REST.

IN THE WEEKS TO COME, ALIA IS WELL CARED FOR. SHE HAS MANY VISITORS.

THE FLAMES RAGE ON, DEVOURING The fire keeps burning, destroying

HEAP OF CASCADING large pile of falling

YOU'D BETTER You should

SHE'S HAD A STROKE. She is very sick.

BEFORE YOU MOVE ON...

1. **Simile** Reread page 26. Alia says that books are like people to her. What does she mean?

2. **Cause and Effect** Reread page 27. What causes Alia to have a stroke?

LOOK AHEAD Read pages 28–32 to find out how many books Alia helped save.

CONTINUES HER RECOVERY keeps getting better
ADD UP TO are

ASSISTED BY THEIR MANY HELPERS Helped
by many people

CHALLENGE AHEAD OF HER BEFORE SHE RETIRES
job to do before she stops working

**OVERSEE THE DESIGN AND BUILDING OF A
BRAND-NEW LIBRARY** work with others to plan and
build a new library

FUND-RAISERS people who collect money

GIVES HER BEST EFFORT TO HER LABOR OF LOVE
works hard to make the new library

Alia's story is just the latest chapter in a long and fascinating history of libraries in Iraq and the Middle East. Here are some other stories you might not know . . .

- The land now called Iraq was actually the birthplace of all written language. Over 5,000 years ago, in approximately 3500 B.C.E., the ancient Sumerians used split reeds from local marshes to make wedge-shaped markings on tablets of wet clay. When baked in the hot sun, the clay held permanent impressions; we now call these writings "cuneiform." Collections of these cuneiform tablets made up the world's first-ever libraries.

- The ancient Middle Eastern city of Ebla, in present-day Syria, had an extensive palace library, with over 15,000 clay tablets stored on wooden shelves. The entire city was destroyed by Akkadian invaders in 2250 B.C.E., but in 1980 an Italian archaeologist **stumbled upon** over 2,000 of the clay documents **still intact**!

    How did these tablets survive over *4,000 years* of nature's wear and tear? After all, of over 500,000 texts held in the great Alexandrian Library of Egypt—built almost 2,000 years after Ebla was destroyed—absolutely *nothing* remains. Both libraries were burned to the ground; what made such a difference at Ebla?

    The difference was that the manuscripts in Alexandria's library were papyrus—thin paper-like scrolls made from stripped, pressed plant stalks. Much like paper, papyrus burns very easily; the blaze that destroyed the Alexandrian Library in the late 200s C.E. turned its collection to ash. With Ebla's clay tablets, though, fire only baked them harder, making them even more durable. By burning Ebla down, its conquerors unknowingly *protected* the city's literature!

- The story of the burning of the great Baghdad library, the Nizamiyah, which made such an impression on Alia as a child, occurred during the Mongol invasion of 1258 C.E. In only one week, Mongol leader Hulagu Khan **ravaged** almost all of the city's thirty-six public libraries. Legend has it that so many books were thrown into the Tigris River that the water ran blue from their ink.

- The Nizamiyah library was severely damaged but not destroyed by the Mongol invasions. In fact, it still stands today, the third-oldest library in the world. Alia's library, too, has survived hardships. Extensive repairs to the Basra Central Library are currently in progress. The library will **undergo a complete refurbishment, paving the way for new services** such as a computer lab with Internet access and a summer-school program for local children. Most importantly, though, the library will continue to house the tens of thousands of books Alia and her friends worked so hard to protect, the precious cultural history of Iraq.

....

ravaged destroyed

undergo a complete refurbishment, paving the way for new services be completely rebuilt and will include new things

BEFORE YOU MOVE ON...

1. **Sequence** Alia helped save 30,000 books. What happened next?

2. **Cause and Effect** Reread page 32. Who was Hulagu Khan? What effect did he have on the books of Iraq and on Alia?

....

stumbled upon found
still intact that were not destroyed